AF253434

Tellwell Talent
www.tellwell.ca

ISBN
978-0-2288-8257-2 (Hardcover)
978-0-2288-6770-8 (Paperback)
978-0-2288-6771-5 (eBook)

to those rejuvenated by the silence of the moment,
empowered by thoughtful words,

...

penned for tomorrow's reflection.

Contents

friend

my friend.
a friend I never had ... thought you should know.

patient beyond measure,
kind without fault,
and
perfectly gentle.

in awe of you.
feeling numb in a place of great wonderment.

your belief in me is
unmatched,
unreal,
and
unimagined.

missing You

been missing you.
at times it feels like too much,
then I think of how much you mean to me
and
it makes senses for a time.

thinking,
believing,
if I don't hear myself say it,
then for sure it will get easier.

it won't always be this difficult.

I am sorry for not letting you know.

asking myself is this normal
to be missing someone this much?
'cause it has never happened to me before.

are you missing me?

morning Vibes

gray skies,
misty rain,
a day designed for warmth.

wrapped in you,
lost beneath our duvet of love,
drenched in desire.

traveling the world in our dreams,
together,
intertwined in each other's shadows.

purpose

pondering what's next for her.

she lives in gratitude, thankful for the lessons learnt.

humility is where she beginnings.
building a future
while paving the path less traveled for other women.

empowering,
enlightening,
and
endeavoring to live a life of no regret.

determined to make a difference,
one moment at a time,
she is purposeful.

I am witness to her greatness!
a beacon,
a light,
a woman who redefines confidence, love,
and
life.

she is where it all begins
and
where it all ends.

life

life is episodic.

gifted with the present,
the caption at each threshold,
the moment between today and yesterday
will read

...

"and it came to pass."

'twas that Moment

she fell again,
the moment he happened.

a kiss to the cheek
awakened that which lay dormant.

a new day began that night
as the sun began to rise.
as it was setting,
the nightfall became daybreak.

she fell
the moment his eyes said hello,
and
his arms wrapped the arch of her back.

alone

you are the only person
I want to be with,
when I am
and
desire to be alone.

finding his Voice

the attempt is made

to silence him,
to make void his experience.

footprints
that participated in the dance
are now center stage,
and
he is persuaded to forsake
yesterday,
to pretend it never happened.

his future
presumptuously interrupted
with assumptions.

questions!
conclusions?

forgone inscriptions chiseled into tablets,
absolutes archaically formed incorrectly,
fiction appears as factual,

misinformed
and
misrepresented in thought,
made audible by unfamiliar lips.

he screamed inwardly
retreated outwardly
and
disappeared
for a moment

(selah)

appearing as he intended

(selah x 2)

who is he?

he is evolving confidently,
charismatically positioned
and
seated gracefully.

intentionally quiet.
poised neatly,
finding my voice
atop this stage called life,

learning when to
and
when not to.

Mrs. MacDonald

so, here's the thing!
I never knew I mattered,
then you whispered
"Thank you for speaking up!"

I thought me,
my experience,
was secondary to everyone else.
who am I kidding!?
my experience was never validated
until you,
you congratulated me for speaking up.

I remember being silenced,
reprimanded for other's bad behavior,
humiliated,
'cause no one,
and
I mean no one, would believe my words.

catching my breath,
tears cascading,
overwhelmingly interrupted by the unbelief before me.

meeting you
developed a self-confidence that I never had.
I remember seeing glimpses of it,
but it never stayed around.

as it flickered,
giving light,
hope was ousted by familiar voices,
so-called loved ones.

You rescued me,
and
I am grateful.

freedom

he never met anyone like her.
she made him better,
wanting to be better,
and
he realized he owed it to himself to be the best.

he liked the man he was becoming.
confident in his skin,
unearthing talents that he once buried
putting them to sleep because of
...
fear.

was it my fear or them other's fear directed at him!?

he awakes,
wanting to become more,
endeavoring to invest the rest of his days
in appreciation.

no more pretending.
the mask is off
and
he is secure.

airmiles

hesitantly he approached her,
scared that he would be reprimanded
again.

to his pleasant surprise,
he sat in disbelief because she believed him.

he cried!
actually, he wept!

crying because it took someone who he thought would
never pay attention,
who had no need, really, to believe him,
affirming
and
confirming that he did matter;
propelling him into a future that he never had the audacity
to dream.

he is
who he is;

he does
what he does;

he is
where he is;

because she gifted him with a new identity.

a reality,
built on the assurance
to be intentionally present
in his life.

appreciating Her

limitless beauty,
picturesque plains,
mountainous land that extends for miles,

beautiful by design
her byways,
highways,
streets,
roads,
avenues,
boulevards,
...
he prefers the long scenic path.

listen to her
as she paves his appreciation
for the road less traveled.
he is attentive to her timing,
the rhythm of her touch,
her pulse at each destination.

landscaped to precision,
cull-de-sacked by design.

intelligence is her resting place,
confidence an effortless cadence,
and
her presence permeates the moment where once
she breathed.

her windows open,
creating a stream.
as tears river into her ocean,
her warmth is therapy.

corners creviced softly,
smooth to the touch,

her hedges perfectly browed,
hills,
valleys unite to one perfect line,
dimpled elegantly.

a stretched canvas marked by her journey,
breathtaking,
and
she is beautiful!

listen to her;
his mind hastens deliberately to her thoughts.

slow down,
'cause in this moment
she is first.

invitation Unanswered

I am being patient,
waiting for the knock to the opened door.
the mirror blurs.
a mist-like film appears.
overtaken.
streams quietly descend.
the distractions.
attractive as they be.
I am anchored.
the sunsets
and,
I remain dressed.
if only the morning would hasten its steps.

un-Sure

am I this priority that you speak of?
why do I get the last few seconds of your day?

am I the most important part of your day?
the person you write of, penciled in the last slot of your
"if I get to today" list?

if I am all that you say I am?
why am I sitting here alone?

ruined

she ruined him for the better
and
he was made stronger.

his introverted mind renewed,
dependent on her extroverted gentle conversation.

his predetermined flaws
separated him,
somehow being different from the foreknown norm.

she celebrated him
past,
present,
and
future,

breathing life into an existence of perceived worthlessness,
reborn to conquer
mediocrity,
an intolerable foe.

transformed

she obliterated his grand ideals,
wanting to become.

he's in vigilant pursuit of a new grandeur,
of being
that which he was designed to be.

he was ruined for the better.
she recognized the magnitude of the man
silenced by fear,
doubt,
the insecurities of others,
silenced by the noise of others' expectations.

he ran frantically home.
the front door was opened,
as if his arrival was a sure expectation.

his tiring journey found rest in her embrace,
locked,
cuddled comfortably.

his poise lay affectionately still atop her beating heart.
the tranquility of the moment,
disrupted by the slight warm breeze of her whisper:
how was your day?

nestled

she asked:
where did you come from?
why are you here?

I came to find you.
I am here to love you.

both are learning what love is
and
how to love themselves in each other.

she is designed for him.
he is the best part her day.

un-Recognizable

the persons they met
and
the persons they are today are different
yet the same.

the person she met
and
the person he found are profoundly different,
vaguely similar.

somewhere between meeting her
and
him finding her,
he found himself.

the person he is today is not the person she met.
she introduced him to a version of himself
that he likes,
and
for that they are grateful.

you are Home

I awake in my dream
twenty-five years younger,
clothed in the wisdom of today,
and
I am with you

equipped with new knowledge
needed to celebrate you.
holding you delicately with
every fiber of my being,
I am excited to be home with you.

time seems to hold me captive.
camouflaged as the responsibilities of
becoming,
initiated to its scheme,
my feet find me running home.

my extremities slow me down.
my heart escapes its posture
pounding through my chest,
reunited,
and
I am awake.

I was never asleep
'cause I will be forever speeding my steps
should we part
to once again be home with you.

it's in Everything

timing is everything!

tick, tock, tick, tock
drip, drop, drip, drop
left, right, left, right
open, close, open, close

Everything takes Time!

falling

in her most vulnerable state,
she fell in love with him

again.

loving him in the valley,
strengthened in despair,
fortified by the struggle,

they climb,
standing atop this mountain called life.

he will love her,
devoted to her.

his friend.
her breath.
their love.
their forever.

devoted

in love,
devoted to you,
realizing now
this path ... though familiar,
had never been traveled,
and
for that I apologize,

wanting only to be known by you.

reNEWed

it is overwhelming
'cause he never allowed (thought to) himself
to consciously
and
intentionally go down that path.

as surprising as this may sound,
he's never been on this path,
'cause nothing is familiar.

nothing compares,
and
everything is new.

on Call

I am awake.
my thoughts are with you,
hoping you are feeling better
asleep,
allowing your body to replenish itself,
rejuvenated,
asking God to ensure you are ok.

I am dreaming,
loving on you,
trusting you are feeling better
awake,
nourishing you back to optimal health,
satisfied,
praying always for wisdom to serve.

the Gift

goals II dreams
wants II needs
being responsible can be costly.

overhearing her conversation,
mitigating the parallels,
his voice interrupts her hesitation.

… get what you need, we'll figure it out …

who is this?
he is someone she never knew existed.
for her?
his voice is new.
his intention?
is her gift.

solitude

it is lonely here without you,
and
I've prided myself as he who enjoys his solitude.
the noise of being alone I would trade
to sit quietly with you.

truth

is there someone else?
surprised by the question,
he responded quickly:
no!

after an honest introspection,
his answer was overturned to an absolute
yes!

yes, there is someone else.

me!

disrupted

disrupted by the new reality of
life!
love!
becoming?

love,
life,
disrupted the day for the better.

to Be

longing to be
held
loved
appreciated

to be more than just a
conversation
causation
introduction

to be wanted
on the journey
purposely placed
positioned intentionally

enjoyed!

replenish

though you were not here,
I fell asleep with you
last night.

I awoke with you.
the weight of your softness
lay atop the caress of my arms,
wrapped in our duvet of warmth.

we enjoyed breakfast
and
then we ate.

dreaming

thoughts of you
interrupted my sleep,

so real
they opened my eyes.

realizing where I was,
I rested my sight
and
there you were.

un-Announced

she enters the room
and
everything changes.

I feel things differently.

emotions, as fleeting they can be,
I am focused.

she has my attention as I stare out the window.

our conversation seems to have begun
before our hellos.

as a baby's gaze,
I am intrigued.

resting on her breath,
has my journey ended?

repentant

lying awake,
searching for the truth,
tossing,
turning,
wrestling with unforgiveness,

the enemy of freedom,
and
he is tenacious,
relentless in his pursuit,
kneeling in submission,
and
I am postured to pray,

freeing myself
of this template called perfection,
chiseled into thoughts
of acceptance,
and
I am free to live,

forgiving my past life
and
its experiences,
the faces,
the names, become a distant blur.

my steps,
immediately lighter.

forgiveness.
a new acquaintance.
praying,
awaiting the day
we become
more than friends.

restored

her steps are quiet.
her intentions need not be discerned,
the surety of each deliberate step.

darkness hastily disappears,
pretending to be in conflict.
the path is made visible.

her gaze
softens the leathered texture of his heart,
tenderizing the soft space
she intends to live in.

she is purposeful.
each brush stroke colors the walls,
giving new color to each cemented brick
meticulously placed to protect his safety.

her smile
commands his attention
and
as he pretends,
not noticing, her gentle touch
taps open,
once locked in famine
by the drought of authenticity.

she breathes
and
he is made alive.
in this moment he is renewed.
hope,
trust,
and
respect unmask his face,
revealing the smile she helped to bury.

old becomes New

banished to the basement
and
after years of neglect,
this once upon a love was left alone.

its dual design no longer served a purpose
until ...

... we tried lifting it to higher ground.
surprised by its weight
and
intrigued,
the inquiry began.

may I have it?
this is going to its final resting place.
may I have it?
why?
what's the cost?
it is to be discarded.

I will take it!

torn fabric,
springs peeking through,
sponge brittled by years of neglect,
but
I sensed its worth.

framed with wrought iron,
its girth solid wood,
my eyes rested on a masterpiece in need of a new
and
renewed purposeful overhaul.

wrapped in white,
piped
and
buttoned in navy blue,
this old love beamed new.

to my surprise,
the once upon a time owner
would reclaim this denounced garbage.

what was the cost?
starting over,
presented with the gift of aloneness,
re-evaluated,
and
now invaluable.

3:00 a.m.

lying awake,
no longer asking why?

separated by
streets,
highways,
byways,
avenues,
boulevards,
crescents,

roads traveled by the masses,
cul-de-sacs of plenty
and
insufficiency,

multiple cities
sharing the same land mass
though addresses differ.

I am awake
'cause you are awake,
connected at the hip.
though never united,
and
we breathe alike.

the night's sky shares the same palette.
stirring quietly,
my thoughts no longer racing frantically
for answers.

I now know why I'm awake,
in sync
to the day we lie awake
together.

intimacy

It might not be all we thought,
were told
it would be,
nor be for that matter.

maybe it is everything we thought it should be
but never thought it could be
because we were never initiated to its potent simplicity.

then she appears,
and
it is nothing like you thought,
were told,
nor dreamt it could be.

for him, she is truth!

in purest of form,
her embodiment is unrecognizable.
she is the unveiling of everything he is
and
everything he is yet to become.

she births life
'cause the person she sees
is the very person he thought?
he had successfully buried.

for her, he is love!

he is not the place, thing, or person
she thought she could easily recognize.
his actions resemble no one she knows,
and
his intention frightens her realization of who she really is.

they cannot be explained,
defined,
nor
illustrated.

for it is an experience!
recognizable only to those who wear the cloak of
vulnerability.

home

I am loyal,
devoted to you,

not because it is required,
a judicial ceremony of appointment,
the right thing to do,
a societal agreement.

what else is there?
who do I go searching for?
when my heart has synced its pace to
your rhythm.

you are home,
commanding my every attention,
my ideal place of adventure,
rest,
and
serenity.

to experience anything else
void of you
is time well wasted.

wanting to do everything,
satisfied doing nothing
as long as I am with you.

I am home.

she said, Yes!

glimpses of her thoughts appear,
entranced in what she says
and
the how.

words emphasized delicately,
altering the course of the preconceived notion,
measured by the volume of her conversation.

her attire is inaudibly expressed.
clothed deliberately,
wondering
is he paying attention?
her intention is not to interrogate;
however,
if unnoticed the investigation begins.

strip-searching his thoughts,
the dialogue unfolds:
the tension,
the moment.
concealed stones boxed to precision reveal
his truth:
his intent is for a lifetime.

enthralled,
lost for words.
pondering the outcome,
the timing of his voice,
together with his calculated disposition.

he is never not paying attention.
she now realizes she is his favorite subject,
the ancient of days being his teacher.

...

because of her,
he knows love.
she is love!

because of him,
she knows love.
he is love!

jealous

me?
no!
absolutely not!
I'm not that type of person,
as if 'twas a curse or character flaw,
some type of plague that the others suffered with
...
that was never to become a mantle I'd ever wear.

then she happened!
waking up that morning,
to the note,

post an assessment
that I'd somehow unconsciously participated in,
the diagnosis stared back at me,

oblivious to its potency,
and,
upon introduction,
jealousy made its presence known.

with the wind knocked out of my feet,
I fell to her humbly.
dazed by her strength,
knees buckling,
I submitted in repentant state.

silenced by her strength
and
profound knowledge,
I now realize
I never had the opportunity to meet her,
or maybe
we were never properly introduced.

adult Learner

staring at the ceiling,
knitted brows,
should I have?

memory serves to remind me of what was.
it's not the necessity of the question.
maybe it is to ponder!?

it cannot be changed.
still haunted,
marked by question symbols,
it propels me to the present,

appreciating the now,
applauding the path of yesterday,
'cause in this moment I am able to appreciate
her feet,
her baby toes,
new footprints.

as we path a new beginning,
knowing the ugliness of days glimpsed in the rear view,
I smile at the beauty of her presence.

yesterday had to happen.
fortified with the knowledge of her worth,
time is priceless.

I am learning.

as If

It's amazing to sit,
to share,
and
to listen.

your shared thoughts,
stories,
and
intuitions

shared,
presented back to you by those with whom you shared

... as if their own.

sometimes

it is sometimes best to be silent.

not everyone has the capacity to understand,
and,
in some cases,

they do not need to know,
and,
or,
lack the ability to understand or help.

sometimes.

contentment

it is a warm day
a surprisingly busy place to park
replenished
and
I gaze
a whispering smile

people laughing
families
togetherness
expectant mothers
fathers holding the tiny hands wanting to explore
old friends
new friends
budding relationships
the communal exchange of vows
celebrations soon to be toasted

it would seem my life through its eyes is at a STANDSTILL

a familiar voice appears
and
I smile

my heart races
and
I am alive

hello
and
for a few minutes
I am noticed
I am full.

need to Know

It's not that I do not care,
nor is it
that I do not want to help.

...

I'd like to be reassured
that you want it more than
I want it for you!

intent

at times
and
in some cases,
it is not the why
nor
is it the who.

the who you are changes the essence of any space.

you affect this space.
between the heart
and
the mind,
a.k.a. the will.

the will causes him to do for you,
and
the why,
in most cases, cannot be explained,
and
is embedded in one word.

love.

promised Land

dreams,
aspirations,
personal goals
sometimes ... cause us to relocate,
separating us from those we love
and
from those who love us.

distance:
time seems to always be plotting,
cosigning,
and
conspiring to keep us in isolation.
...
maybe,
just maybe,
that is the formula to the promised land.

being alone can be painful.

life teaches that the real pain
is in an unfulfilled purpose,
the unrealized dream.
therefore,
we must persevere.

only then will we conquer,
fighting to leave the world a better place,
one dream,
one goal,
one day at a time.

do you Dream II

awakened to the night's skylight,
stars shining,
flickering in their brilliance.
the moon lights the sky,
and
its reflection slow dances atop the ocean's stillness.

her fragrance lingers.
flames dance to the aroma,
as the silence invites me to sit.
the night
and
her breeze encapsulates my thoughts.

giving thought to her beauty,
my eyes smile, staring at His gift for me,
reflecting on where I am,
and
the moment.

I am thankful for each experience that has positioned me to know,
appreciating the importance of now,
understanding that it was a necessary course.
she has become,
and is,
my favorite subject.

nestled comfortably in the stillness of the night,
her warmth is comfort.
breathing effortlessly,
the rhythm of her heart is steady.
on the off-beat I share my thoughts,
laying each track to its ideal tempo.
she is His Masterpiece.
I am custodian,
curator,
and
student;
attentive to each lesson.

as the moon takes her rest,
the sun greets the morning.
as the rain showers to begin the day,
its invitation is subtle.
as we lay intertwined in our embrace,
music makes her entrance,
and
we dance.
our morning feels new.
class is already in session,
and
I am present.

appreciating the moment,
I am in awe of my responsibility.
to learn, I must.
to learn, I will,
and
I am intentional.

I will not accept any less than my best,
learning to listen,
with my soul's purpose to
understand.
however,
a few days in detention I will gladly serve,

reminiscing on the path that led me here.
silencing the whys?
overtaken by it all,
looking into the rearview mirror,
I am able to appreciate the crossroads,
detours,
and
conflicts
that have me at your side.
positioned to serve,
I am student,
teacher,
and
scholar.

the night's rest once again does its magic.
she is awake.
I am awake,
aroused by the magnitude of the moment,
attentive to the high altitudes that invite me to climb.
exploring ... I am reminded to replenish
for the journey
Home.
it is difficult to be attentive
when hunger pangs lie waiting,
and
breakfast is served!

mornings have taken on a different meaning.
in its appearance,
solitude has its importance
and
knows its
boundaries.

her presence, however,
in any given moment,
is a welcomed pause.
she presents to restore,
an intermittence.
the gift of time celebrates our union in the present,
and
she has my undivided attention.

no sense Pretending

as inevitable the night sky,
the weather does change,
and,
for a time,
it will work in your favor,
but it will storm.

as your disguise disappears,
the unrecognizable gives birth,
and
neither one is the benefactor.

time does ask the question,
rhetorical as it may be,
gives place to uncover
truth.

beauty of Rejection

one of life's best gifts
removing the excess
where once it posed as invaluable.

its process reveals a hidden treasure,
unveiling priceless parts of you,
providing clarity to a vision obscured by untamed desire,
unrealistic expectations.

life introduces an unrecognizable you to self,
meandering a path to untapped potential,
introducing you to a better version of self,
and,
through the debris of it all,
stumbling into the beauty of who you really are.

...

remember to say thank you.

slow Dance

I dream of us dancing,
lost in an inaudible rhythm,
syncopated to our heart's song,
held closely by a fretless score.

she is music,
the orchestra of my playlist,
postured to untap the virtuosity of life.

her song gives birth to an unrealized gift
suspended in time.

the Journey

in our efforts to celebrate its significance,
measured by a dash that separates the beginning
and
the inevitable,

its linear design
is outfitted with never-ending winding paths,
hills,
and
valleys.

storms threaten its very existence.
cloudless days exalt the vastness of the heavens.
time governs us all,
and
with each step reminds us to be present.

we learn to our advantage to:
appreciate the good in the midst of the bad,
cherish the midday sun in the darkest of midnight skies,
and
enjoy the summer's heat in the midst of the frostbitten winter.

semi or Detached

while enthusiastically finding ways to celebrate you,
you were secretly designing a plan to live my dream
somewhere else.
returning to your place of complacency was home,

disbelieving the known truth
that you would not return to the dreams of tomorrow.
moments shared seemed devalued,
discarded as worthless.

journeying with no explanation of why to help inform the
how seems heartless;
somehow, it seems that was the plan.

insecure

he walked away, thinking
he wasn't the most eligible,
that,
he somehow didn't measure up.

he would eventually not be the chosen one.
he made it easier on himself to choose for her,
and
he knew the conversation had started.

he took the proposal as confirmation to disappear.
he was unsuccessful in his efforts to erase her.

he thought the replacement was your better choice.

taking Notice

my heart's cry is that we all posture ourselves correctly in
our lives,
realizing there is purpose in everything we experience,
taking nothing for granted.

We are created to serve
and,
to not be exploited.
And,
while earnestly seeking to uncover the reason for our
existence,
taking notice of things that propel us forward

as created beings connected to the creator of it all,
hesitating not
to respectfully ask why or why not?
listening always to the path that opens the continuation of
our footsteps.

there is an Expectation

I often hear these words, "I do things with no expectation."
time
and
observation
have provided me with the reality that this is not entirely true.

as we water our plants,
feed our children,
love on loved-ones,
there is an expectation of growth ...

we might not expect the same output as our input;
however,
there is an expectation ...

growth happens in many forms
and
ways.

make no mistake,
and
there are no exceptions:
self-growth is not exempt!

uncertainty

rest in the moment of uncertainty
to once again be in a place of hope,
'cause
it will all make sense
in preparation for tomorrow's past.

love Note

as the morning awakens,
your feet touching the warmth of the floor,
step into this new day
knowing you are loved
and
a gift to the world.

invaluably postured,
praying that yesterday's smile
travels with you always,
and
the aromatic gestures of love
consume your day,

anchoring your heart
where thoughts become alive,
void of promises.

love

an expression of love is
acceptance,
intentionality,
and
consistency;

a gift to keep on giving,
intentionally wrapped,
ribboned with the will to give life.

time gives life its value,
an appreciation for its
present,
past,
and
future.

growing Up

learn to be whole,
to love,
and
to be loved wholeheartedly.

whole!
not to be confused with perfection,
with the capacity for
growth,
void of capped limitations;
imperfections pave the path to uniqueness.

ascension

her ascent into the afterlife
paved a new path.

navigating the terrains of his anger,
she did not instigate, neither did she need to mitigate.

choosing a higher altitude preserved the truth.

him now learning that his misdirected self of pious pride,
stoic misinformed disposition,
and
misappropriated position
held him alone.

his owned words built him a fortress of solitude,
a place called home,

hidden behind a wall of fear with no one to visit,
rooms filled with absence.

best Friend

being with you reminds me of my childhood;
savoring my favorite meal,
eating small portions to prolong the experience,
and
preserving the taste
till we indulge when tomorrow begins again;

my denim cap that wears with everything,
my favorite sweater
and
to any place;

whether in hand,
or tied around my waist,
sitting by the dryer to embrace its newness again.

regression

growing up,
learning before I could speak,
color was ascribed to a thing,
never a person.

migrating north,
thinking before I would dare speak,
color was an easy descriptor,
not the best
as once perceived.

living the reality,
observing our lives in so many shades,
an easier path does not equate to a better outcome.
it shortens everything,
regardless of how far we have come.

never have I

pondering what tomorrow holds,
now realizing
never have I witnessed,
understood the beauty of devotion,
nor felt its conviction.

giving myself completely,
surrendering my will seemed more spiritual than physical.

being reserved wittingly seemed cautious.
now realizing
pretention disguised itself as worthy,
seemingly you would detect truth deciphering my heart's
intention.

the truth is
never have I lived authentically.
learning now that love never postured itself as a noun,
reverbing itself always in tangible action to give.

in the midst of it All

tomorrow has a mind of its own,
assuredly.
enjoy life in the certainty of now.

yesterday cannot be repeated.
in the midst of now
is only when life happens.

good, better, Best

I am good when I am alone.
really,
I'm only recharging.

I am better when I'm thinking of you,
making plans for us.

I am best when I am with you,
even when
doing nothing.

hello

patiently waiting for us to meet,
united again to celebrate us,
and
fortified with the mind to serve,

not bound to extravagance,
however,
the moment is priceless.

appreciating our lives
as they change our hellos to "good morning",
"have a great day!",
"how is your day?",
"how was your day?",
"I miss you!",
and
"sweet dreams".

reality Check

we exhaust ourselves in the what if,
ignoring the gift of the here
and
now.

everything has a cycle,
operates within seasons,
and
in every season there is work to do.

restrain judgment in any (one) season,
'cause the good you see today
you might not see tomorrow,
and
yesterday's indifference
only lasted the seconds you witnessed.

alone (the gift)

at some point,
in the midst of the busyness of life,
he recognized his tiredness,

weary from being alone,
surrounded by so many who called him friend:

friendships,
relationships,
and
courtships.
yet amongst these vessels,
he drifted alone.

anchored to a port
named delusion,
bunkers left in desolation,

retreating from the fight.
unrecognizable smiling faces,
arms extended,
shouts of warm exuberance
swiftly grazed by him
to those with outstretched embrace,

disappearing into the noise of the crowd.
making his entrance to home,
its threshold, though familiar,
opens to the quietness of a peaceful sleep
and
he is alone.

respect, trust, security

there's no hierarchy present,
none more important that the other,
intertwined
yet
distinct,
a symphony that holds each musical note as one.

providing the sustenance for the journey,
love is the air we breathe:

respect,
trust,
and
security.

the earth which grounds us
is the foundation,
bedrock
to withstand the storms of time.

life

a blank canvas?
a coloring book?

a blank canvas!
a coloring book!

regardless of your posture of punctuation,
your tools of artistry,
what may present as a well-designed opportunity
requires your participation.

choose from the spectrum colors,
color within the lines,
create your own lines.
however, you choose,
attendance is mandatory.

in that moment, you decide to follow the instructions.
make your own interpretation.
there may be consequences.
will it be your masterpiece?
who determines its signatory value?
time will tell,
but
you got to begin.

seasons

everything happens within its season,
a spoken reason,
and
there is a predetermined reason
that requires work in every season.

resist the urge to cast judgment on anyone,
including self,
or
in any one season.

timing is everything,
and
everything takes time.

be present in your season to be consciously aware,
paying attention to what comes next.

the bounty
and
the texture of your fruit is dependent on the quality of seed,
and
the environment where it is planted
determines its survivability.

alone (the gift) ii

realizing he was tired of being alone,
he removed himself completely from all the ships.

sound bite

honor,
respect,
and
protect the sacredness of your nakedness.

... it's not only the physical.

not everyone should know nor deserves to know
your thoughts,
plans,
and
dreams,

past,
present,
and/or
future.

the Affair

introversion was his invaluable gift.
the joy of missing out was not a shared response in the
presence of those who he thought mattered.
image was to them a perfect reflection of things,
lacking intelligence.

the affirming eyes that took notice,
misplaced innocence
and
immaturity,
masquerading themselves as youthful.

time colluded with knowledge,
and
wisdom resided in a timely disposition.

for him, morning awoke in the midst of the day
as the light that gave way to the mind took notice.

intrigued by the experiences that resulted in this moment,
self-preservation that once followed from a distance
was now center stage.

the farther away he stood,
the more its shadow decreased.

consumed by a familiar scent,
and
dependent on the direction of the wind
drawn to the volume of its voice,

attentive to the timely resonance of a dream,
it began,
and
he fell in-like with an irreplaceable peace.

comfort

a comfortable bed,
a warm pillow to lay her head,
and
she longed for home.

belonging has become a distant memory.
relevance has vanished where once the newness of life
flourished with excitement.

being reminded of who you were,
wanting to forget,
gives opening to a place where she'd rather be assured.

past lessons.
experiences.
not realizing the voice was befriended in that very moment,
relived in the potency of words once buried.

love covers,
protects that which it betrothed,
and
she questions if its strength is secure.

knowing the actions of yesterday carry a weight noosed tightly
and
are crippling,
wanting to escape the isolation that yesterday has built.

the deed never penned her name.
her eyes never reflected the figure that
blueprints her reality.
she was never part of the equated conversation,
and
she begins again.

that's the way it is

sometimes you do,
sometimes you don't,
and
that's just the way it is, sometimes.

gestures

it's the soft, warm caress of her hand
palmed gently on the back of his head.

in that moment,
he is strengthened with the knowledge
that he is loved.

the Hibiscus

her roots,
original to the tropics,
uprooted for her diverse beauty
from the sunny isles to the frigid north,
forced to climatically survive his frosty breath,
displaced to suit his palace.

her intelligence,
capped in servitude,
unhinged for the exploits of the academically inclined,
forced into submission.
her body used to make wise,
and
the ungrateful few rich.

her blossoms
provide sustenance, whether hot or cold.
uncovered beauty threatens the very veins of each sect
'cause when she awakes,
the sun rises in its brilliance
and
the moon provides its comfort.

her diversified beauty
none can describe.
she is an experience,
a lesson,
and
a moment in time.

her colors,
too powerful to remain silent,
her voice volumes throughout time,
copious by design,
natured in resilience,
and
she is renewed in spring.

her tenacity unbothered,
driven by her desire to care,
she blooms despite the climate.
time celebrates her as hero,
and
to celebrate her we must.

life's Surprises

it's the imperfect moment
that creates a lasting impression.

it's the unplanned experience
that endears a new path.

it's the untimely lesson
that cradles a new beginning.

save for later ...

there will always be someone waiting
to see you fail.
it will present in the disappearance of congratulatory words,
in the sarcastic cheers,
and
in the thunderous silence of applause.

comments shared behind closed doors
will find their way,
and
your disbelieving ears will echo uncontrollably,
as best friends,
befriending allies,
sail to share their fortune.

in the midst of that discomfort,
an unfamiliar voice appears
and
silently whispers the support of an army.

in that moment,
the verses memorized will emerge,
and
from the dark recesses of your mind,
you will begin to understand.

it is then,
and
only then,
that the passages recorded
will appear as alive with truth
as your naysayers become the engineers to their well-
designed snares,
entrapped in regret,
and
positioned to see you rise.

uncertainty (reverb)

the uncertainty of the unknown
brings with it less anxiety
when you trust the One who created time
with you in mind.

becoming comfortable with not knowing
provides the space for miracles,
which in time
place you in the midst of contentment
and
supernatural dependency.

a Thought

life begins
when you no longer desire the approval of others.

affirmations and conformations
no longer
define or decide
the authenticity of your day.

likes and dislikes
no longer
dictate or fluctuate
the emotions of your evening's rest.

dancing with You

I'm listening,
dancing with you,
caressing the arch of your back,
awaiting the softening of your posture.

I'm listening,
dancing with you,
leaning into each moment as the beat fades,
words now synced to the rhythm of your breath.

I'm listening,
dancing with you,
grasping the soft texture of your pawn,
as your eyes now communicate the desire of your heart,
and
your lifeless body is renewed again.

tomorrow

tomorrow patiently waits for you to decide,
unhurriedly unveiling its intended plan
and
timely revealing the process:
a synchronized pattern
you could neither determine nor detail.

its design complements the path you choose,
positioned to respond,
seated still.

its intention is to never interrupt your actions
but confirm your intent;
the day reflects in-kind.

oblivious to its attributes,
it aligns with purpose.
personal conviction to become
distinguishes needs from wants,
urgently unsatisfying the opportunity to merge
another's design for your path.

everything becomes visibly achievable,
manifesting itself.

you becoming that tangible design you envisioned,
equipped to change your world,
boldened with humility,
dressed with the knowledge of who you are,
influenced to make a difference.

a Moment

he asked,
"what was the best gift you ever got?"
I responded softly,
"you!"
thinking I misunderstood his question,
he responded, *his voice slightly amplified,*
"no, dad! what was the best gift you ever got?"
I responded,
"you, Ethan! you are the best gift I ever received."
he then stared at me,
and
we drove quietly to the airport.

p.s.

wanting to see you thrive,
with or without me,
recognizing the importance of your smile.